FADED VOICES

SERENITY AYMALA

ISBN: 9798986381305

FADED VOICES

WRITTEN BY

SERENITY AYMALA

CONTENTS

Introduction

Have you ever considered what happens to untold stories or to those who weren't given a chance to share them? Do they just fade into the background? Are they passed on even if no one knows of them? Some are placed within us to teach a lesson. Some are meant to make you think or feel in a way you've never imagined. Others are truly experienced. Regardless, these stories deserve to be told, to be heard. Are the stories forgotten about as those behind them soon will be or do they have an everlasting effect? Think about it...

So many different variations of emotions come over me. There are so many different causes. How do I gain control over these emotions before they gain control over me? Can they be changed? Should they be? These are just a few of many questions rattling around in my head. So, just how do I feel? Well, often times I find myself feeling drained. I also feel scared, angry, betrayed, and hurt. With all of that flowing through my veins, somehow there is still hope in my heart. Am I just blindly hopeful?

I sat out on a journey to possibly answer some of these questions and to ease away the eerie feelings that lurk over me. This journey is bigger than me. It is spiritual, emotional, and mental. So again, I ask, how do I feel?

Drained...

Verb   past tense of drain. (of feeling
or emotion) become progressively
less strongly felt.
2. deprived of strength or vitality.

Drained…

Over the years so much of me has been given and taken away. Very little has been understood or appreciated. Nothing has been reciprocated. I had to be a woman before I was able to be a girl. It was always expected of me to do and be better. Never was I allowed to have a mishap, though many would come.

I had to have it together and do the right or proper thing at all times. Lord forbid I grew tired or weak. I was considered less than or stupid. I would be spoken down upon and to. If my attitude wasn't just right, I'd be told that I was this or that and such negative things would happen to or come upon me later on in life. "You're going to get beat up in school." "Someone is going to hurt you one day." Or one of my personal favorites, "You're never going to have friends or get married."

Of course, those are just the perfect statements to feed a child's brain and self-esteem (sarcastically speaking of course). It is important to be very mindful as to what you plant into a child. What is planted, in most instances, will grow. Comments such as those are mentally and emotionally draining. They scar the very existence of not only a child's self-esteem but their entire outlook on life as a whole.

So instead, plant a seed of power, growth, positivity, strength, and knowledge into your child. Do this, watch, and be amazed at what is to come. Bare witness to what that seed grows to become. What is sent out will return back to you. It is mostly up to you as to how. Whether positive or negative, it will come back. We all know this as karma, but I like to call it the boomerang seed. Ask yourself, would you eat from the tree that you've planted?

Growing up felt like an uphill battle. Continuously fighting. Fighting against the naysayers, negativity, stereotypes and family issues as well. The more she grew, the more it seemed like the relationship between she and her mother dwindled away. She would go through so much that a kid would run to their mother about, but she was unable. Or at least she felt that way. She had to bury it all inside. Never able to discuss it nor fully heal from it. She just had to continue to push on.

It was draining. How much she felt that she needed and wanted understanding was draining. No one could ever understand or even imagine. No one knew. It was her against the world and yet all she ever wanted was someone. Not just anyone but her specific someone. Her one. Someone who would come walking her way and complete her. Someone she could love and trust. You know, someone that she could grow with, learn with and from. She'd thought she found him, only she would later come to realize that it wasn't really him that she was looking for.

Her love… her love for him was just too much. Too much for him and too much for her. It turned from love to obsession. Not obsession over him, nor sex, nor materialistic things but the feeling. The feeling of being loved. Of being wanted. Of being needed. The intimacy of it all. She obsessed over it. She had to have it.

She never knew what it was so to think she'd finally found love was indescribable. She put too much on him. He didn't deserve it. She gave to him what she should have been giving herself all along. She deserved and desired the love and care of a man because she had never had it before.

Daddy issues... Her stepdad was never really around for many different reasons and her biological father wasn't even given the chance for reasons, apparently, she'll never know. So, when he came along, he seemingly filled a void that she didn't even know existed. She needed him.

Only it wasn't him, it was her father. Her dad, she needed him. She still does. She knows that the past cannot be rewritten nor undone but she still wonders. She wonders what it would have been like to have him. She wonders what he would have taught her.

What would he have said to her when she was scared or nervous? What would he have said to her when she decided to date or felt heartbreak? What would he have done? How would he have comforted her? She always wanted to go to a father-daughter dance too.

Well maybe they'll dance together in the sky when they're reunited again in the future. She still needs him but he, once again, can't be there. It's not fair but know that she'll be okay. All that she asks is that he please helps to guide her. She needed his guidance before and somehow, she needs it even more now. She gave someone else the love she needed from him.

Daddy issues... She doesn't regret it because it taught her the lessons that she feels she would have learned from him. Maybe in a different way, of course, but she learned. She will continue to learn but please don't let her go. I can't let you go. I was barely given a chance to hold onto you so please hold onto me. Don't forget me, I won't forget you. I will teach your grandchildren what I was able to know of you and what I learned from you.

I will call upon you in another way since there's no phone number to dial Heaven. Please hear me. I need to hear you, but I'll find another way for now. Just don't let me go. Daddy issues... I hope that you know that I have no ill feelings for you and that you are missed. Your grandson looks like you, talks like you too. So, thank you.

I'll take that as a reminder, as a blessing. You could have taught them what I cannot. You could help them grow up to be men. I'm forever grateful that my sons were able to meet you before you flew away. Although, it hurts because they won't remember. As I had to live the same.

I had you as a baby but lost you before my memory could serve me. I gained you again as a young adult but again you were taken away from

me. Still, the small amount of time we shared
together will forever be cherished. I will be honest
and admit that the void is still there. Your passing
touched all of my wounds. The burn I felt, I feel. I
have so many questions.

I was so angry, held resentment against a
few and was so hurt. I still hurt. You filled a portion
of that void, so I guess it's up to me to determine
how the rest will be filled. With love, I'm sure. At
least this time, I'll know how to go about it. I won't
look for you in another. I'll love me first and
foremost. I'll love my children above all else.

See, you're doing it. Even from the skies,
you continue to teach me. Thank you again. I really
appreciate you. Tell God that I see what He did
there. While you were here, while you were sick
and suffering, I used to say that if I could take that
pain away from you, I would. He gave me my wish.
You're no longer hurting but now I hurt. It's
bearable though. I hurt differently than you and I

am definitely okay with that. I'll endure.

Daddy issues... I hated losing you when I felt as if I had just gotten you back but all things happen for a reason, right?... Right? Finally, this little girl has become a woman and it's honestly, though painfully, due to my daddy issues. I wouldn't trade it for anything. A gem. A gem you were, a gem I found, a gem was bestowed upon me. I'll treasure it always. Daddy issues... I'm so grateful for them... for you.

Though I am grateful for those issues, I am also still learning from them. Learning how not to instill them into my children and subject them to the pain that I have felt. No one could ever understand. Many may talk, but until they have walked along this path, their talk will remain just mere words. We cannot control how children are affected by the things that we do. We just know that it will happen. We can influence but not control. It is best to do exactly that, our best. Do our best by our children.

Despite any past issues between their father and I, I could never hurt them the way that I've been hurt. They deserve so much better than that. They will not be surrounded by negativity, lies, secrets, toxicity, nor dysfunction. They did not ask to be here nor are our issues their issues. I will not project our adult issues onto my children.

I have seen firsthand what the mistakes of elders can do. Everyone knew but no one ever said a word. I was forced to go through life living a lie. I was never even told that my stepdad was not my biological father. I found out for myself, the hard way.

I never knew that my parents were married, never even knew my father's name until years later. All I ever knew was my stepfather, whom I am grateful for and loved. So much of my life remains a question. So many of my questions remain unanswered. Even as an adult, there are parts of myself that I will never know.

I was unable to meet any of my paternal family. My father's parents as well as most of his siblings have unfortunately passed on. I have no family history. I do not know if maybe some of their ways, interests, and etc. were passed down to me. I don't even really know much about my father's life.

More importantly, I have no family medical history to refer back to if, Lord forbid, anything were to happen. I do know that my father had type 2 diabetes but that is all. Yes, that is very important but what else? What about other family medical issues that may be hereditary as well?

What about having and feeling the love of my family members? Why was I denied that? Why was I denied my father's embrace, his love? I am unsure of myself at times due to these things. It is the minor details that we tend to overlook that make the biggest difference. As the saying goes, "it's the little things in life." They may seem minor to others but they have lasting effects.

Still draining... scarred. You could never understand the damage that has been done. Verbal, emotional, mental, and physical. Every time your voice was raised unnecessarily, letting her know how much of a bother she was to you. Every single time your day was rough it somehow was her fault, or at least you made her feel that way.

Even if things were going well, you'd find a reason to be upset with her. You'd find any and every reason to fuss and fight, to demean, to lay a hand on and shun her away. You disowned her a many of times. So many that she almost felt as if she was never yours.

Never derived from within you. She would cry and apologize so many times but it was all so draining. Why couldn't you be there to wipe her tears? Not even one. She would have given anything to feel a simple embrace from you, let alone a warm one. What did you want from her?

What did she do to you? Why are your life's mishaps and mistakes for her to be blamed? All she ever wanted, all she needed was for you to be what you were meant to be through birth. Craving the love of a parent that seemingly hated you was a huge burden for her to carry; it still is.

Draining. She is so sorry for whatever it was that you had gone through and for whatever it is that you are still going through. She prays for your breakthrough. Please breakthrough. Not for her but for you. There is this beautiful being below the surface awaiting your approval to be free. To breathe. To live. Yes, she knows this battle is difficult. You've forced her to fight it with you, for you. Though, it was never her battle to fight in the first place.

Still, there she was. Always on the battlefield. Fighting for a love and relationship that she had grown to believe she just didn't deserve. She didn't deserve, but desperately needed it. Why can't you see that you've played a major role in draining the life and love out of her? Something that you, especially, should have been planting inside of her for herself as well as the generations to come.

You feel drained… but know that you are capable. Know that no matter what comes your way, you will overcome.

Scared...

Adjective   Fearful; frightened.

Never knowing what stone would be cast out against you can cause you to live in fear. Anxious. I tried so hard to make my family proud and to keep us together but it felt like it was never enough. Like I was never enough. No matter what I did, it never seemed to amount to anything. Or at least that's how I was made to feel.

I played a role. You know, I had good grades in school, participated in sports, and was very active in the church. You would have thought that I stood out and in a positive manner, but I was never really noticed. Never was I the girl out in the streets.

Although I had been exposed to so much, and at a young age, I stood my ground. It's amazing to look back now and realize that there is so much that my family doesn't know. We see the wilderness of the streets on television and hear about it in fictional stories and etc. but no one respects its reality. Yes, I was afraid. I beat out just about all stereotypes against young girls who look like me.

Though it was a struggle, I still got it done.
Why don't we hear more about this? We always
hear, see and read about the stereotypes which are
unfortunately, glorified. Glorified and judged but
never corrected. They are usually misunderstood or
false altogether.

Sure, we know about the media's portrayal
and other nonsense but what if the truth is discussed
more? What if we voice how we got to where we
are and why? Let's get to the root of the problem.
This is why I am scared. What ever happened to
communication and healing? What is a young child
to do when something happens to them that they
know no one will believe or they know will be
brushed under the rug?

What happens to the girl whose family
member and friend of the family tries to or does
touch her? How does she speak up? How is this
child's voice heard when no one pays attention to

them until it benefits themselves? She's so adorable when she sings in the church's youth choir. She's an angel when she dances on the praise dance team. Oh, it is so amazing the way she effortlessly flies through the air when playing sports. Everyone's so proud of her when she breaks records and gets all good grades in school. "Yay, that's my baby!" "That's my girl!"

Yet, if that's your precious baby then where were you? When she needed you most, where were you? When she lost her virginity to a stranger who just so happened to be a friend of the family, where were you? When she sat there bleeding, shaking, and crying while alone, did you think of her? Oh no, of course not. You don't even know. Do you see a pattern?

Again, she found it funny how a lot of people around her, especially those closest to her had always assumed the worst. Everyone talked about how she was more than likely promiscuous. If only they knew. They saw her body and how physically fit it was. Oh, because that automatically meant that she had to be sexually active.

She always thought that maybe exercise, a healthy diet, as well as you know genetics, gave those results but what does she know? It was just HER body. The most insane part of it all was that she herself never saw what others saw. She did not think she had a nice body, figure, or pretty face. She never thought highly of herself.

She never learned how to wear makeup or dress up nicely. She mostly just went with the flow. Whatever felt comfortable to her was always a yes. Due to sports and having three brothers, she was also a bit of a tomboy and it showed. Whenever she looked into the mirror she only saw a small and thin girl. One that definitely went unnoticed. Or so she thought...

The red truck. What about that red truck? She could never forget, though you'd never even remember. Just a normal day for siblings to walk to school. The objective: get to school safely and return home the same. Except, not everyone agreed with that notion. The red truck, it appeared out of nowhere.

The young brother and sister duo carry on toward their elementary school but then there it is. A red pickup truck starts to follow them. They keep walking, I mean what else are two very young elementary school children supposed to do? They were only halfway to their destination.

The distance from home to school was maybe a mile or so long beginning in their neighborhood and then walking alongside a busy road. Yes, they were alone. As they were every day. Except, they weren't. They mentioned the truck to the authority figures at their school but once school was out, the children were on their own. This would happen for two days. The second school day began and ended the same.

They began their journey home, and once again, halfway through, the truck reappears. This time, getting closer and closer. The driver opens the window and offers the kids a ride.

They say no and keep moving. The driver offers again and again before putting the truck in park in the middle of the street. He gets out of his truck and runs up to the kids, grabbing one by their backpack on their back. The siblings yell for the man to let go but he doesn't.

So, they fight him off, take off their backpacks follow through with their plan to separate and prayerfully make it home safely; if at all. The younger brother runs off as told by his sister. She distracts the man, kicks, and screams until she's free of his grip and able to run away. She runs in the opposite direction of her brother so she doesn't lead the man to him.

She zigzags through the neighborhood until she loses the big red truck, then she runs home. Her brother was there waiting safely. Thank God. They call their parents and the police but by the time anyone arrived, the red truck was gone. That was one of the scariest moments in their young lives.

Though it all happened so fast, they'd never forget it. A big, red, pickup truck. That red truck followed them in their dreams for months. Did you comfort them? Do you ever check on them? You never even mentioned it again after it happened. Did you forget about them? Hopefully the man in the red truck did too.

The girl didn't know it, but she would grow to get used to that feeling. I bet you're wondering what happens next, aren't you? What else happens with her? She wonders the same...

What happened to the girl who's one true love no longer loves her? Yeah, sure these things happen right? What about when he decided that it was okay to abuse and use her? When even those close to him would try to as well. She can't tell her family because they'd look down on her and speak negatively on her name and character.

All of her personal business would be spread like a wildfire but no support would be given. I guess it's safe to say that she didn't tell her family about the very scary miscarriage she suffered through alone. It never ceases to amaze me what is said about a woman. Oh, she was probably this way or that. She was more than likely having sex since a young age and with a lot of partners.

She just got caught up. She probably didn't even have a miscarriage but just went to have an abortion. It was a food baby and not a real baby. The stories go on and on. "She just wanted someone to feel sorry for her." "Why was she with him anyway?" "She's stupid, she knew that he was no good."

"She allowed him to put his hands on her." "I would have left a long time ago." "I would have done this or that." Oh, how easy it is to speak when you don't have the mic. When you're not in her shoes, it is easy to say what you would have done but what about her?

That question probably isn't allowed though, is it?

WHAT ABOUT HER?

You are scared… but know that you are in control. This is not your ending, but your new beginning.

Anger...

Noun

A strong feeling of annoyance, displeasure, or hostility.

Verb

Fill (someone) with anger; provoke anger in.

I, I mean she, is so filled with anger! Tears flood my eyes whenever it crosses my mind but still, who can I turn to? Who would even care? What about me, I mean her? The blind often times sees more than what is let on but chooses not to acknowledge it. The dark cloud of negativity, accusations and assumptions is looming over her soul. The inaccuracy of it all.

No, she was not an easy girl. No, she was not having sex at a young age. She did not even lose her virginity until she was a young adult and halfway finished with college. Even if she had been, would you not acknowledge what introduced her to it in the first place? What about the family member that tried to sexually assault her? Right. I forgot we tend to hide the truth in fear of what "others" would think or say.

So, is she just supposed to pretend it never happened and move on? Her body still pained from that. Her soul still cries out. With fists balled tightly, she presses on. She carries it with her everyday but at least she still carries on. She's so strong and doing so well that you've already forgotten about her, haven't you? You may have forgotten, but she is still angry.

Is she just angry alone or is she running? Running. It once was her escape, her coping mechanism. What started by force to keep her busy, turned out to be exactly what she needed to ease her.

Her mind as well as her body. Run, run my love, run. No, not from anything but to what she wants. To what she needs and longs for. She runs for strength and understanding. Run, girl, run. Years have gone by and still she runs.

Many practices, many track meets, many schools, and many summers. So much blood, sweat and tears have been left out on the track. She was once forced, but now she loves it. She needs it. It has become the only source of therapy she'd ever know. All she ever knew to do was run. She worked so hard and for so long.

She overcame so many obstacles and endured through every ounce of pain she felt. The girl wanted to go far, despite being told that she couldn't, being doubted, being left out, and having very little to no support.

Here it is, senior year and it's her time to shine. All of her hard work would be put to the test. She had already climbed the mountain, now it was time to leave her mark. She was working to earn scholarships as well as run track in college. She had gained the attention of many universities and now she just needed to do what she felt she did best, run.

All of a sudden, without any warning, she is sent away from home. Away from her family, in the middle of her senior year. Before her senior prom, and while needing to be there to earn what she had worked for.

Here it is, no, there it was. There it goes. Gone. Everything that she had worked so hard for, gone. The new school where she was sent did not allow transfer students to participate in sports. She lost it all. In the blink of an eye, it was all gone.

Disappeared into the darkness, out of her sight, out of her grip. What was she to do? She couldn't give up. She was right there. She had it. It was in the palm of her hand, then quickly snatched away. The question that she would never get an answer to was, why?

What was the purpose of her being sent there in the first place? Sent to a place far from home. Somewhere she had never even heard of before. Alone. Her dreams taken away from her. It was unfair but such is life.

She had no idea that this would be the start of many heartbreaks and unfortunate circumstances to come. All at the hands of someone she should be able to run to, but she would learn to run from.

Her anger, it was growing inside of her. A monster was being created. She would try her hardest not to give life to it but it seemed unavoidable. Anger. She was filled with it, surrounded by it, and soon consumed by it.

Broken. Not just angry but broken from the anger. Beaten down and feeling defeated but still not giving up. Angry! She does not want to be filled with anger but here she is.

Here is yet another story of yet another negative experience that will anger her. She is having a hard time understanding the mental state of others. She found herself questioning it often. How can a parent claim to want what's best for their children but then everything in their power to keep them down?

They expect their children to do and be the best but treat them like they are the worst. Their children are talked about as if they the spawn of satan. If they are, then what does that make you?

Whatever happened to "what happens in this house, stays in this house"?

Your child at times, had to walk on eggshells around you. Being careful not to trigger you. They always felt as if they couldn't be themselves. You would literally demean them. Instead of encouraging them, building them up, and guiding them, you tore them down. Bit by bit, day after day. You wanted to change them so they fit into the picture you had inside of your head.

Why weren't they good enough? You were always there for others. Supporting, speaking positively about, and helping everyone else but never your own. Idea after idea would be shot down. No support was ever shown. At times you'd turn away as if you didn't even see it. You wanted their lives to revolve around you, meanwhile you acted as if they weren't apart of yours.

They are angry! So angry but a word would never be said. It happened so often that it became normal. It was just how things were, right? If ever they attempted to voice how they felt, they were told to stop with the "poor me syndrome". Wow, who knew having emotions like a regular human being would be so frowned upon? They bottled it up inside but no one knew that their bottles were only being shaken up.

Their explosive reaction thereafter would be seen as crazy and toxic. They were even called selfish. Wait, they're selfish? For wanting love and support from their parent? That makes them crazy? She had heard enough. Enough was enough! Actually, it was too much. Wrapping her mind around what was happening was impossible.

There was no way. Did it really happen? Was she just having a nightmare? She'd hoped so but was ready to awaken. Please wake up! She tried to pinch herself but unfortunately, she wasn't dreaming. It was oh so real. Unbelievably real and she'd had enough. Angry wasn't the right word to express what she felt, she was pissed and rightfully so.

Wait, why is she so angry? How dare she walk around with an attitude after everything that she had been through! How dare she be upset or show any emotion due to her experiences and treatment thereafter!

The audacity of this young woman to be angry with her family and friends for wronging her and speaking down on her. They spoke and spread around false statements but she'd be wrong to feel any resentment due to it. Do you still see the pattern?

Unfortunately, it is those closest to you that will hurt you the most or show you no support. What a sad day and age we live in. We're so caught up in appearances that we allow the unthinkable to happen and never be dealt with. Now her anger is just another stereotype. All of this just to save face and hide, but from who? From what? What are we hiding from exactly?

What are we so afraid of? Ourselves? Our own abilities, our powers and strengths? What if we embraced them instead of running from them and allowing others to dictate our potential?

We live in fear when, in reality, the only force that can defeat us, is us. Why do you think it is one of the highest objectives on the agenda? A person is expected to remain silent through their pain and yet somehow be unaffected.

We have got to change the narrative and outlook. In order to do so we must first correct ourselves. As the saying goes, it starts within. If we continue to bury our experiences and the emotions that come thereafter, we are further hurting ourselves.

We have control over our outcomes even if it seems as if we don't. Our skies may look dark but we are our light. We just sometimes need a reminder of this. Though it will try, do not allow the world to dim your light.

Shine. Shine in spite of. Shine throughout. Shine because "they" don't want you to. Shine simply because you can. That light was placed inside of you for a reason, even if you are unsure of what that reason may be. Do not allow your anger to become who you are.

It was a side effect but will not be the final outcome. After years of lies, confusion and rocky experiences, the anger inside of her had been built up like a brick wall. She has plenty of reasons to be angry but she has to decide to overcome her anger before it takes control of her. We all have a choice. Choose you.

For years she wandered aimlessly looking for someone, something to make her anger go away. She tried it all and mistakenly projected her anger onto others at times. Buried. She was drowning herself in these negative emotions and finding herself buried alive. She just couldn't seem to figure it out. What was she supposed to do? Who was she supposed to be? How could she possibly get passed this?

She ran and hid but she knew eventually she would have to face what was to come. How could she press on like this? It was simple. She couldn't. So, she became what and who she thought she needed to be. The person she thought could get her passed her mountain.

The issue was, she failed to realize that she could not simply pass it. She needed to face it head on and climb over it. It would take a lot from her. She buried her emotions and put on a front, a mask.

The mask. The mask that she wears as she stumbles through life is one of a kind. Much like the woman behind it. What a mask. A mask so tough that no one notices it. Though she may be hidden, her anger cannot be contained forever. What will it take? How long? She patiently, as well as fearfully, awaits the day that her anger comes bursting from inside her like the waters behind a broken dam.

It was held together for long enough but no longer. I am angry but my strength is still unwavering and unwavering it shall remain. Even in my anger, I've learned not to become it. I am angry but my anger is not I. As I work to overcome it, I build myself up.

We must learn to grow from our past. Never allow your anger to control nor ruin you. You did not come this far and fight through so much only to defeat yourself. You are allowed to get angry as long as you learn to channel it in a positive manner. Channel it and never lose focus. She's learned. She does not wish to be known for her anger but for her strength and knowledge.

You are angry… but know that your anger is not who you are. Anger did not make you, so do not let it break you.

Betrayed...

Verb Past tense of betray.

Expose (one's country, a group, or a person) to danger by treacherously giving information to an enemy.

Treacherously reveal (secrets or information)

Be disloyal to.

1. Unintentionally reveal; be evidence of.

Betrayal is the breaking or violation of presumptive contract, trust, or confidence that produces moral and psychological conflict within a relationship amongst individuals, between organizations or between individuals and organizations.

She was just a young child, her memory may not be clear nor accurate. She doesn't know what was happening. It's not expected of her to remember this. She will get over it. Right? No one ever seems to care or even consider the damage that is done to a child through their words or actions. Throughout our adult life, it's unfortunately the same. Due to us being adults, what we think and feel is overlooked.

Often times, adults are ignored in that aspect. We're expected to be tough and show no emotion. Do not react to anything but turn the other cheek. We're sensitive and attitudinal otherwise. If it's extreme then dare I say, we're considered ghetto. We're put through hell then turned on once we make it. Oh yeah, we weren't supposed to make it. So now we're the problem.

The betrayal. I've been through so much and honestly, I wonder how I am still here. No one has ever bothered to apologize but will in turn use my

pain against me. Whether it be a friend or foe, it
mattered none. My past and hurt is revisited and
thrown up for discussion and entertainment.

Or maybe even just so someone has
something to talk about and feel relevant. If ever I
mention the smallest of my pain or experiences, I'm
talked down to and on. One tiny pebble compared to
a mountain of truths but you cannot handle it.

So far I have come, yet so far I still have to
go. This journey isn't over. It is only the beginning.
The beginning... it's almost comical how many
times I have reached this stage. So why do I still
feel as if I have gotten nowhere?

I started but never finished. No, not by
choice but life just kept pressing pause when all that
I wanted was to press forward. Looking back on it
now, I should feel betrayed. I worked so hard for so
many things but have yet to bear the fruit of my
labor.

I blamed and beat myself up for years,

though I'd never show it. As mentioned, my dreams with running track were taken away from me. I did continue on to college but after my freshmen year, I fell sick. So sick that I had to have surgery, plates put into my face, etc. Here we go again, being held back. It was no one's fault but it was killing me inside.

My sophomore year came and passed without me. So now there I was, a year behind. After having to move back home and my family relocating, I finally went back to school. That feeling of finally being able to finish what I started and accomplish what I wanted was indescribable. I was on cloud nine.

I rented an apartment near campus and was off to the races! Oh, but of course, this beautiful thing called life would show its face and many talents. After having no interest in dating, I somehow found myself in a relationship. I was in love. Crazy and blindly in love.

Of course, every relationship has its ups and downs. So, I went through a bit of drama and it affected my schoolwork but I pushed through. Never failing a class nor missing a beat. That was until my father fell ill.

One day while preparing for a test, I received a phone call telling me that my dad had a stroke and was found unresponsive. The university that I attended was a few hours from home so I had to drop everything to be there. He was hospitalized and due to him not being married and me being his eldest child, all of his affairs would fall onto me.

In the event that something should happen to him, it would be my call as to how we would proceed. I had no idea what to do nor how to do it. To be honest, at this point, I didn't know if I was coming or going.

Suddenly I was caught up in a world wind of emotions and legal documents but I had to do what was best for him. He'd been in a coma for some time now and everyone around him were thinking and telling me to prepare for the worst. I had done exactly that but was not giving up on him.

Apparently and thankfully, he didn't give up either. Although, I had letters written to my professors from both myself and the doctors, it wouldn't be enough for me to be excused from and still maintain all of my classes.

Again, the betrayal. There was one class that I unfortunately failed, and of course, it was a required course that I needed toward my degree. I lost those credits but we had my dad back. With that being said, I believe the trade was even. Though, it had a big impact on me. Over time my dad grew stronger and was back home and to himself again. I went back to school and continued on.

Things were back on track. Yes, there were all sorts of doubt and negativity being thrown in my direction but this wasn't a first. I knew that I could handle it. After all, look at what I'd just made it through.

I, however, found myself now one year behind and having failed a class that I would have to retake. I was already dealing with a lot but according to life, it just wasn't enough. What's a girl to do? No, seriously...

What's a girl to do? Once accused of "getting a new family" after being given the cold shoulder and left alone. I'd say that is shocking. While in college, she worked at one of the on-campus restaurants to pay her rent. After the school year ends, most employees are let go because business slows dramatically, if not shuts down, after all of the students return home for summer break.

She was one of those students. She had already paid 2 months shy of her entire year's rent. After the school year ended, she was no longer working and could not afford her last two payments. She was also having car trouble so her money was completely spent.

Due to her getting a ticket for an expired tag, her family decided not to help out to teach her a lesson. Due to lack of payment, her internet would be turned off, then her water. Not to mention, she had no money to eat and ran out of groceries. So, there she was, stranded hours away from where her family lived at an apartment that she was now being evicted from.

Oh, and with nowhere to go. No help. She couldn't even call because at the time she was still on her family's cell phone plan. Again, to teach her a lesson, her cell phone service was turned off. With the internet being turned off, she could not use her Wi-Fi either.

She was forced to pack up her entire apartment and stuff everything into her car that was unable to be driven. Her ex-boyfriend's mother found out she needed help and sent a bus ticket so she could come there. 2 days later, after begging a neighbor for a ride to the bus station, she was on her way. Now, because she allowed someone else to step in to help, she was being accused of replacing her family.

Wow, just wow. What's more, she endured some of the most embarrassing and depressing times of her life. There was a time where she'd considered ending her life.

How did she get to this point? Why? All because of a traffic ticket and unforeseen circumstances. Completely disowned and alone. A TRAFFIC TICKET! Again, not for speeding or doing anything crazy but simply over an expired tag. Did I mention that the ticket was thrown out?

It was beyond heart breaking and gut wrenching. Especially given the fact that she wasn't the first nor the only child to get into legal trouble. They were always immediately bailed out and helped. Their business may have been told and themselves talked about but never were they neglected.

Wow, so imagine how I've, I mean she's felt all of these years? It doesn't matter what I have to say because you want everything to be about you. You cannot get over you to see me. Which is why you've missed my entire life thus far. Even when you were there physically you were absent mentally and emotionally.

You failed to realize, but it was painfully noticeable. No hallucinations, just ignored and untold truths. My secrets, the few I did reveal, were thrown back in my face. Which is why only few were mentioned.

If only they knew. The smallest grain of salt thrown would burn my core. Every person I've ever loved has hurt me in some way. It was those closest to me that stole a part of me that I'd never get back nor recover from. To this very day, they continue to do so.

My love and desires used against me. The only focus is them. It has always been them. So, for me, it's my turn. My time. I've taken on more than my fair share of grief due to others only to suffer alone. Why must it always be suffering? I've grown from the resentment I've held against some and wanting revenge. For others, not so much.

They only think of me when they want to attempt to use me or are in need of something. No more. I've dealt with more than the average person, yet I say nothing. Of some, few know. Of none, do they care. Though it'll be used to attempt to weasel their way back in when they want attention.

It is profoundly obvious, but they believe otherwise so around and round we go. This evolving door needs to be shut. I've gotten off of the rollercoaster. Do not pretend to care only when you hear of a tragic event, yet you cause me just as much grief on your own terms.

Despite my grief you've still pushed against and tried to hurt me, or take advantage of situations. Though it didn't work, you tried. That's what matters. It's the principle. Things are so easy in today's time that they're complicated. One cannot tell another how they truly feel without doubt or fear of them feeling that way for or entertaining someone else that they have access to.

With the growing access to others, we have less access to self. Also, less and less access to reality. Access is freedom and yet it is the very thing that has our minds in chains.

The betrayal. The trust was broken and lost long ago but life ties us together. Now I am forced to deal, but make no mistake, I have learned. Even when it doesn't appear to be so, I know. The worst form of betrayal though has been my own. The betrayal of the heart. My heart and mind are rarely on one accord.

Despite everything, I keep forgiving which allows others to feel as if they can try again and again to repeat the past. I also fail to hold onto anger and feelings of betrayal. I've grown to truly hate some but the love I felt will always overpower that.

It makes no sense. How can I not hate these people who deserve nothing less? Yet, I love. I'll never look at nor interact with them the same but I love them. Like a damn fool. What has changed from the past? It's simple, me. I no longer act on my emotions whether positive or negative. I do not show nor allow it to affect my decisions. I refuse to take a step backwards when it took years to overcome this mountain.

I once read a meme that said, "I have so many places to go but backwards isn't one of them." That must be one of the truest statements right now. I will not allow my heart nor past love to betray my mind nor spirit. That is over.

You feel betrayed… but know that you matter. Know that you are worth it. Love yourself the way you've loved everyone else.

Hurt...

Verb   cause physical pain or injury to.

Cause mental pain or distress to

(a person or their feelings)

Be detrimental to.

I don't matter, or do I? Lost, confused and craving the truth. Crying myself to sleep night after night, tossing and turning only to find no comfort. A painful smile and a broken heart, hoping for the best and not seeing it. Feeling unwanted and like I don't matter.

Hurt and lonely inside, a feeling I know all too well. The tears continue to flow. Of love is what is spoken, but the feeling is lost. Yearning to be held; to be loved. Of honesty and reality is what I seek. An open hand never to be held, a heart never to feel warmth.

A touch never to be felt, all alone through the struggles of life. I can change, I can stay calm. I can have faith and learn to trust, but the pain and lies are undesirable. Being there only to be left alone, giving all of me only to receive nothing. Feeling as if I don't matter. Words unspoken, a path not yet traveled. Of silence is what I shall speak, hold it all in.

Cope on my own, forget it all. Adapting to this empty feeling, maybe I should leave. No turning back. Strong but in pain; unforgettable past and experiences. I love too hard and care too much. Maybe I should let go, stop caring.

Keeping to myself, after all, I don't matter do I? Despite my faults, flaws and insecurities, I have a purpose and will fulfill my dreams. Not giving in to distractions nor negative emotions. Feelings of self-doubt will not defeat nor define me.

Nothing said to nor about me will stop me. Keeping my eyes open and head held high, I can get through this. After all, I matter, I always have.

As you know, I'm no stranger to pain. We're not friends but aren't exactly enemies either. Just familiar territory. I grew tired of hiding behind my smile and pretending that the pain isn't there. When I'm not numb, the pain is all that I feel. I walked around smiling, seemingly joyful but no one heard my screams from the inside. No one noticed the shattering of my heart. I was dying inside. Tears are my footprints in the sand. They show me how far I've come and from where. They help me to not lose my way.

It is ironic that one of the things we do not want to do is sometimes what we need to do to as a reminder. I've fought through tears a many of times, attempting to hide the hurt that I was feeling. As if my eyes aren't the window to my true self. Still unable to be open about my experiences, my diary has grown full. I've held on to so much, bottled it all in. I fear the breakage that'll take place when I've reached my max.

Although, I do look forward to it. It is a necessary period to go through but it is absolutely frightening. Will I come out on the other side of it? Will it swallow me whole? Will I lose myself like before? Wanting and needing to be loved, accepted, and appreciated but failing to do it myself, for myself.

I hurt myself by leaving my happiness up to others. I wanted more than anything for my family to be whole. To create happy memories and leave lasting impressions.

Instead, the scars on my heart show me that we do not need everything that we want. Ironic, family should be a must not a maybe. I've struggled to accept what is, though, when things are out of my control. Hurt, my other half. We have literally become one. It often seems like I know nothing other than this.

I was once told that though I'd been through hell, I never show it. I show no emotion and I never cry. If only they knew that for years that's the only way I've gotten to sleep at night. Tell me this isn't life. Tell me this isn't it for me. The one I once thought was it, was more foe than friend. Ran off with my love, something you didn't even want.

You've come back time and time again for what you don't want but know she needs. It was just something about the feeling. It hurt more than anything but gave a sense of intimacy that she had been craving. The only intimacy she'd been given, even if it wasn't pure. The momentary excitement and being held was enough. It gave her back what was lost not long before.

She can never forget what she went through, what she bled for, what her body experienced. An unforgettable loss. A lasting ache. The sharp pain piercing my soul. You are the only connection to it. I hurt at the very thought of it and you not being there. I tremble then I feel it all over again.

Hold me, let me go, then do it again. We go nowhere but my mind has been all over. It hurt me to even hear your voice. I hated but needed you. I hate me for that. I'm better without you and will never forget what you've done. You hurt me so deeply that I fear love. My nails painted red with the blood of my broken heart and being hydrated with the many tears I've cried. I believed in love but love never believed in me.

The pain was nearly unbearable. Physically, mentally and emotionally unbearable. My body shook, my mind troubled, and my heart broken. What was worst was being completely alone. You were not there but away with another. Giving someone else what was taken away from me. You smile while I cry. I could barely breathe. I couldn't eat. I couldn't sleep. I couldn't even think straight.

Pain. It was all there was to know. All there was to feel at this time. Attempting to really process what had just happened, what we'd, no I had just lost. You never even cared so the loss became my own. Mine alone.

To this very day she feels the painful ripping and tearing of not only her body but her soul. She could never forget. It haunts her. The thought and picture in her head of that bathroom floor, the towels wrapped around her body and placed on her car seats, that lonely and terrifying drive to see the doctor, the sunken feeling hearing those dreadful words, and finally…the loss. She can never let go of what her body could not hold onto. Haunted.

Hurt. In that moment she needed someone, anyone but there she was all alone. With no one to hold her, to tell her it would be okay, to drive her home, to care for her as she healed. Healed… she never did. Still haunted, still hurt.

The one person who knows even a portion of my endeavors has gone. You had become my rock, my journal. Missing you in my life for eighteen years just to have you for ten then lose you again. Only this time, I can't get you back. I hurt! I went through a lot to have you here and learned quite a bit along the way. You were what I needed, and I still do.

Please come back! Hug me, laugh with me, tell me a story from your past, ask me to go to the store to buy your favorite snacks…say something, anything! Let me hear your voice one last time. No one talks to me the way you did, nor do they try to understand. I didn't trust my secrets in the ears of any other and I still have more to speak to you about. I still have so much to learn from and about you. I had no other to go to for advice.

Who can I go to now? Who can I talk to? Who can teach me what I need to learn? Who will be there along my journey to guide me? I still need you. You left me way too soon. Why does everyone I love end up leaving me?

You left indefinitely. I wasn't ready. I never will be. You were partially the cause of my resentment towards others. I moved on from it but just for you to move on too. Did you have to go? You hurt me. I'm being selfish because I never had a chance to be before. I didn't get the time I needed with you. Then again, no amount of time could ever be enough.

Does anyone understand how I feel? This may sound childish but it is all so unfair. I've buried

more than just hurts from the past, burned more
than just bridges I no longer wished to cross. As we
know, hurt people hurt people. The problem is that
a lot of people do not even realize or refuse to
accept that they're hurting.

Instead, they find ways to maneuver around
the pain, meanwhile passing it along. Pain is one of
the worst and yet most unacknowledged diseases.
So, it is time to climb higher out of the pain, out of
the suffering.

Suffering…my dear, you are suffering. As I've said, there is this beautiful being awaiting your approval to be free. You may believe that you are hated or unappreciated. That couldn't be further from the truth. We've all made mistakes, it's just time for you to let go of yours. Do not look for your acknowledgment at the end of this because here it is…

Do you want to know what I truly see when I see you? I see a warrior. One that has been fighting so long that they no longer know who they are without it. You are at war with yourself. My Love, you've already won. You were always my Wonder Woman. I looked up to you and wished that I could gain even a tiny grain of the strength that you have.

No matter what you faced, you overcame it all. No, life was not always pretty nor easy, but you made it. No matter how long it took, you did it. I am proud of you. I love you so much. I just wish that you understood that. You've been hurting for years and full of fear. Please release it all! You are so much better than what you feel. Let me be the first to tell you that you need no validation, approval or acknowledgment from others. You are and have always been a Queen.

You lost your crown along the way, but I found it. I've learned so much from you, even if it hurt me to do so. It was always something to be learned. My work ethic came from you. You are a hustler, a grinder. You always handle your business. Your children never went without. No, you are not perfect, but you did what needed to be done. We see you. We appreciate you. We Love you.

You finally opened up about things that have affected you. What you didn't do was end it there. You did not heal. You passed your resentment and pain down. Though I may not have agreed with or was hurt by your methods, you made me strong. Even through your flaws you molded me. I've held so much resentment against you, but I get it now. Pain knows no name. It attaches itself to anyone. Detach yourself! You do not have to remain in pain. You are more than that. You are a true Goddess. The issue I see is that you still don't know who you are, what you are. Your strength both empowers and scares you. You've lived in fear far too long.

There's this little girl inside of you trying to find her way. Sounds familiar, doesn't it? She was passed down to me. I became who you were running from. Now, I'm found. You're found. You're forgiven. Now, forgive others as well as yourself. You're not only hurting yourself but those around you who want nothing more than to love you. It's heavy. The weight has become unbearable. They have to go. Let's break these chains!

You feel hurt… but know that you are heard. Know that your voice, nor will you, fade into the background.

Still, We Climb

Verb   go or come up (a slope, incline, or
staircase), especially by using the feet and
sometimes the hands; ascend.

Move with effort, especially into or out of a
confined space; clamber.

Noun   an ascent, especially of a mountain or
hill, by climbing.

An overnight and easy task? Absolutely not. It has taken years and is still an ongoing journey. Growth and learning are never-ending. As long as there is breath in our lungs and activity of our brains, we are capable of change. Capable of learning and growing.

Take it all step by step and day by day. Relieve the pressure and guilt placed on yourself. You have no reason to feel guilty nor be in a rush. We are all human and not one is perfect. We all fall, choose to rise now. Give to yourself the love, attention, forgiveness, and strength that you have been breaking yourself down giving to others. You deserve that.

You need it. Love yourself. Love yourself. Love yourself. You are not here by mistake. Find what brings you joy, what eases you and capitalize on that. Never give up on yourself. You are your biggest critic and also your biggest supporter. Choose wisely as to how you reflect on yourself.

Choose how to represent yourself. You are not weak, broken, worthless, nor forgotten. If motivation escapes you, read. Listen to music that uplifts you. Research ways to help yourself. Begin first with gaining understanding of self. Get to truly know who you are and what you want out of life.

Know that you deserve better than you have experienced. You are not your past. You are not your experiences, your pain, nor your mistakes. You are growing. Continue to do so. Allow yourself to breathe. I know how it feels to have that burning sensation in the back of your throat.

Needing to say something but feeling unheard and misunderstood. I know the feeling of drowning in your thoughts, fears, and pain and being suffocated by them. Breathe. Give life to who you really are. Take on your new form. You are so beautiful.

I have also learned not to cope. Do not rely so much on finding ways to simply "cope" but not heal. It's time to heal. Manifest your healing. Trust your healing. Live and grow through it as well. Block and tune out the naysayers and opinions of others. Know that your opinions matter. Your feelings matter. Your thoughts matter. You matter.

This is your life, your journey, and your vision. No one else can live for you so do not allow them to live through you. Doing so can further your destruction. Live your life for you. If you feel counseling would help, please seek it.

Take time out for self. I found exercise and writing to help me. Write out what you may be afraid to share with others or to even say aloud. What cannot be said can always be written. Even if these writings are for your eyes only. Get it out!

Free yourself of any thoughts holding you down and back. Free yourself! Research and recite daily affirmations. Keep reminding yourself until you are able to truly believe what you are speaking and hearing from yourself. Leave notes around for you to see randomly as you walk throughout your home.

Pray, pray and pray harder. Start and end with prayer. Send your problems and fears up in prayer. Leave them there. We take on more than our share sometimes. Maybe this battle isn't for you to fight or at least not to fight alone. We are never alone, even when we feel alone physically.

Much like when writing, we can say in prayer what we cannot in words. Our tears and silence are understood. They are heard. You are heard. Even when all is going well, pray. A lot of times, with prayer comes tears. Cry.

Often times we're told to fight back our tears and push forward. No. Cry! Let it all out. While you cry, release what is hurting you. Look into the mirror and face it. Yell if you need to. You do what you need to for you. There is no right or wrong way to heal. Just be sure that you are conscious of your actions. Be mindful of self and others. Try not to project your emotions and thoughts onto others.

It may not be your fault that you've been hurt but remember that it is not their fault either. Do not pass that pain, anger, and fear on. Break the cycle. Break the chain! It ends here. It ends now. It ends with you, in a positive manner.

With that in mind, learn forgiveness. Even though those who have hurt us may never admit it nor apologize, we cannot stunt our own growth due to it. Stop and realize that they themselves may not have learned, grown or healed from their past. Therefore, they project those emotions and trauma onto others. Often times it is done subconsciously.

True, in some instances those who do not know how to express how they feel find ways to make others feel it too. Misery loves company. They did not learn how to overcome so they share their pain. We need to be mindful of this and try to avoid those people if possible. Keep in mind that growth is better than avoidance though. Also, do not allow their projections to become your blueprint.

We are not here to pass judgment nor bash anyone's character. These stories are meant to open our hearts and minds. They are meant to correct our blurred vision. To help heal our inner and wounded child. No one is perfect and we all have our faults. Some more than others but we all bleed red. Those who have wronged us sometimes need love more than we know.

It does not mean they are a bad person. They are simply a hurt person who is no longer in control. They've become a lost and emotional being. They may even subconsciously envy you or your progress. Sometimes it is difficult for a lost soul to be happy for another being found. Pray for and forgive them.

We are no longer holding grudges or resentment towards others. Keep the space if needed but work on letting go. For you. In doing so you ensure that even if they appear, your entire mood, atmosphere and aura are not swayed. I am living proof that what you hold onto, will also hold onto you. It holds you back from progressing.

You will find yourself bound and chained by your thoughts, pain, and resentment or, dare I say, hatred for another. Forgive them for you. For your sanity and stability as well as that of the generations to come. That trauma, hurt, resentment etc. can be passed down. It can be completely unintentional but very likely. Again, free yourself!

Walk away a better, stronger, and wiser person. What tried to break you was broken. You are here. That speaks volumes in and of itself. You have already come so far, keep going. Reach your goals, be successful, be happy, find peace and love. That fire in your eyes will light your path.

Keep climbing. Do not worry about slipping, this road gets slippery sometimes. As long as you get back up and fight on, you are always a winner.

You are a warrior. You are a miracle. Know and accept that. You have overcome what others may not have been able to.

Your scars are your beauty marks. Your tears are your breadcrumbs. Never letting you lose your way. Your fears are just your weights being lifted to make you stronger for your next level. Look at you! Going further than you thought, further than once told you ever could. Let that be your motivation. Every step you take is an accomplishment.

Despite the rollercoaster of emotions and turmoil I've endured, I continue to grow. At times I find it hard to look in the mirror or into the faces of others who remind me of what was and, of what was lost. These obstacles will be overcome as well and a new day will arise. Though it is frightening, I will not turn away. I choose to be inspired, to be encouraged by it all. That map shows me where I have been, how far I have come, and opens my eyes to where I want to go.

The beauty of it all is that, still I rise. Sometimes with tears flowing down my face, and other times with a smile. This mountain, I will continue to climb. These hurdles I will continue to jump over. I will not be stopped. In the eyes of defeat, I will not be seen. I know no defeat.

I know no limits. Cliché? Sure, but a false proclamation it is not. I've felt drained, scared, betrayed, angry and hurt but now, those emotions will feel me. Note to self, stop running. I still pray for you, you've got this.

I love you, you're everything you need and you are strong. You are wise and beautiful. You will overcome, you will succeed and you are enough. Day after day I fight through pain, fear doubt, feelings of inadequacy, worthlessness and like no one truly sees me. More importantly, day after day I fight, push forward, and overcome. So, not to self, I'M STILL HERE.

This world will persuade you to believe that you are not enough, you will fail, you aren't important, you have no purpose and that you are not loved. The world feels this way about itself because of the treatment from the people in it. Remember this, the world was here long before these issues were, and so was your purpose. You were created before your struggles and experiences.

You were here before ever meeting those that have wronged and hurt you and so you will be even after them. Your circumstances and feelings do not define you nor can they break you. Only you have the power to do so by allowing the negativity to affect your mind. Life sometimes throws unfair blows. Apart of our journey is learning how to roll with the punches.

Do not give up on yourself. Do not give in to what did not make you. It does not deserve that power over you, so take your power back. One cannot speak for all, but please allow this to be the voice of the silent souls out there. The souls that feel like they have no voice, no say. Or they feel as if no one cares about what they have to say or what they've been through. They may feel as if no one hears, sees or understands them. Or maybe as if the world has turned its back on and forgotten about them.

You are not invisible. You are not alone. I see you. I am you and I am with you. I love you.

Peaceful

Adjective

Free from disturbance; tranquil.

Not involving war or violence.

Peace...

The one thing I had been searching for but had no idea how to find. The ultimate goal was to find and live in peace. To walk in and be at peace. No ifs, ands or buts about it. I had gone through it all, searched high and low but just could not find it. Where was it? Who was it? Why was it? What was it?

I had thought once I overcame the drama, fear and ill feelings from my past that I would find peace. It wasn't until a couple of years later that the lesson I truly needed to learn would come into my life. Not perfection but a mental connection to this lesson. It was sure. It was peaceful. He was peaceful, a bit difficult but peaceful... Mr. Peaceful. I didn't understand it then, but I soon would.

Without intention, I was taught so much about myself and about peace. I learned to walk in my truth. It was in the way he carried himself, the way he spoke, the way he moved. Whenever asked how he was or how he felt, he'd answer "peaceful." I asked how he was always able to be so at peace the way that he was.

His answer was so simple and yet so complex. "I don't let anything bother me and I control the things that I can." Sure, it sounded so easy but without self-discipline it was impossible. A lesson within a lesson. A challenge. One I had been struggling with until he'd said that. It hit me like a ton of bricks. I needed to regain control of myself, of my life.

I had mentioned feeling at peace one day and he asked, "why not every day?" Again, such a simple question but it weighed heavily on my mind, in which I admitted to him. After being asked that question, I had been in a good mood, no, at peace ever since. He made me realize that I controlled my own peace.

Why not every day? That question broke

something inside of me that I had no idea needed to be broken. I had been forcing myself to "keep it together" and hold on thinking that was how I'd reach my goal. If I just hold on a little longer, I would find my peace.

Come on! I can do this! Stay strong, bend but never break. No! No... break. Why should I break? What good would that do? I'd be considered weak if I break, right? At that moment I took a step back and asked myself, "sweetie, how do you think sculptures are made?" Some of the most beautiful works of art are made only through breakage. What may start of as a pile of rock, ice or whatever substance is chosen, is soon broken down into a masterpiece.

It now has purpose. It is now a wonderful site to see. It only becomes that way by chipping away at the pieces that aren't needed. So why can't I do the same? Little by little, piece by piece, break. Break away the pieces of negativity, toxicity, fear, anger, betrayal, confusion, pain, and whatever else that has been holding me back. Break so that I can be molded into the woman that I was meant and desired to be. Being strong is great but be strong enough to let go. Strong enough to heal, to grow, to glow. I can control my peace. I will.

Instead of looking for it in other things, people or situations, I simply had to be it. I came to the realization that I'd been giving others control and power over me. My happiness and peace depended on outside sources. I was in a good mood if this or that. I had a good day if "...". I was happy because "...".

I was not in control. A choice needed to be made. No matter the circumstance, choose to be at peace. Choosing not to be would not change the situation but choosing to be could change the outcome. As well as my overall outlook. No, those words never left his mouth, but he showed me.

In the little time we'd gotten to know each

other, he'd shared so much wisdom and helped
me gain my peace. He motivated me in so many
ways. There were things that I didn't understand or
maybe didn't agree with but I realized that what
was happening was bigger than that. Whenever he
wasn't joking, he was teaching. I always asked
questions. Eager to learn and to absorb it all.
Always taking mental notes and never taking a
word for granted. What I felt was trivial, I took
with a grain of salt.

He mentally stimulated me. Learning how
he worked, handled things and moved throughout
life was life altering for me. I needed that push.
That reminder. As I mentioned before, it's the little
things in life. The tiniest of things can make the
biggest difference.

One small word or act of kindness can truly
change someone's life. At a time where I was down,
stressed, hurting and unsure of myself, in came
peace. No, not the person but what he taught me. A

true breath of fresh air and a needed lesson for sure. He wore a necklace that represented the "key of life" better known as the ankh. I now know that peace is that key or at least a major portion of it.

He has no idea. I will always be grateful for this unexpected lesson. I thank God for it every day. Again, no he was not perfect, but it was the perfect timing, the perfect lesson. I had been praying for guidance, a sign, or anything and I felt as if that was what I had just received. In the simplest of ways, by simply speaking to someone.

God truly works in mysterious ways. Everything that I had been hoping and praying for, manifesting, and working towards was suddenly standing in front of me. He was the living embodiment of everything I wanted for myself. Not in a man. Not relationship wise, but literally for self. I was going round and round again in my head trying to learn how to live.

How to truly live my own life for me. I

wanted to be able to work for myself, start a business, travel, experience and see different things as well as places. I wanted that sense of peace and freedom that he seemed to possess.

He was doing what he wanted, working and living for himself. He was living. God opened my eyes through him. He showed me that what I wanted was just a few actions away. I could have it but I had to be willing to change what I was doing. I needed to make more as well as new moves.

I could have what I desired, do what I desired, and be who I wanted to be. I had always been a source of motivation for others but had never experienced having someone in my life do the same for me. I felt like it was my calling and I loved every bit of it.

It was natural, second nature. Never intentional. That drew me into him as well. He never actually tried to motivate me but he did. It was the small details about him that caught my attention the most. They were what stuck with me, what taught me. Through him God gave back to me apart of me that I had given away to others but neglected to give to myself. I needed that. I appreciate it.

It's funny, we could have crossed paths long before we did but it just never happened. Though there were attempts, I could never bring myself to follow through. I later realized that it just wasn't time. I wasn't ready, mentally nor emotionally, for the lesson that he was sent to teach me. I still had some growing to do and understanding to gain.

After my father's home-going I went through an enlightenment period. It took losing someone I truly needed and worked so hard to have, for me to let go. I was able to hear and see clearly without the pain of my wounds blocking me or influencing what I was experiencing. I was ready for my next lesson. My peaceful lesson.

The biggest blessing throughout all of this

was learning what I wanted others to see. I smiled but was not always happy. The same stands for others as well. As I've said before, just because others seem happy or at peace does not necessarily mean that they are. Again, hurt people, hurt people.

Instead of battling their demons, some dance with them. It becomes a way to cope instead of fighting. We never know so it's so important to slow down and evaluate things, people and situations before assuming.

Listen to your body and spirit. When you feel something isn't right, don't ignore it. Don't put it off, don't wait. Trust your process. I went through hell before and closed myself off from the world. I gained focus though.

I was able to work on myself and build. After a four-and-a-half-year long journey, I finally stepped out and took a risk. I just didn't know the magnitude of that risk. The fear of missing out as well as my own thoughts encouraged me to change. Not only my mindset but how I typically approach situations.

It took some time but I learned. Before, I came out of my shell only to be reminded of why I went into it in the first place. The pain and disappointment that I take with me now, I could never wish on another. Why do we do the things that we do? Why do we make certain decisions? Why do we allow fear to cloud our judgement? What if I walk away in fear but am wrong? What if I was right?

The answer arrived but it was too late. Just a young woman out in the world with little to no guidance. They say experience is the best teacher but she'd argue that pain is. Here she was again, hurting, when she thought she was on the verge of peace. She breaks as she looks into the mirror asking herself why. Why does she always hurt? Why does she keep choosing wrong? What is wrong with her? She looked into the mirror again but related more with it's shattered pieces.

What seemed like a beautiful lesson, was also an extremely tough one. It was time to look at myself in the mirror and acknowledge that I was in my own way. I was my obstacle. Once again, I learned & I grew. I'll never forget but I conquered.

I find peace in knowing where I am and seeing how far I have come. No, I am not perfect by any means but I continuously strive for better. I am no longer who I was. That young girl, naïve, fearful, hurt, and ignorant, is no more. The mental and emotional growth is unmatched. Never ending.

There is always room for growth and knowledge. I grow, learn, and glow more every single day. Even on the days that I may not feel like it. Instead of putting myself down and being too hard on myself, I push forward. The motivation may not always be there but the drive is.

I have finally felt peace and will not let it

go. I deserve it. Not only because of my journey and struggles but simply because I am willing to go out and get it. I choose peace. Today, tomorrow, next week, next year, always and forever more. There is no right or wrong way to go about it, just get it done.

Be grateful for every low, every tear, every lesson that has contributed to your growth. I know I would not be half of the woman I am today without them. I used to be ashamed of my journey. The many times I had fallen. The times that I was not on my feet, living how I wanted, and doing what I love.

Ashamed of the goals that I sat for myself but hadn't accomplished yet. Or the fact that I could not look into the mirror and know who was staring back. I was embarrassed to feel. I rarely shared my feelings. I love hard but rarely. I could really like someone but never express it because I always felt like I was not enough. I was not pretty enough, tall enough, my hair wasn't long enough.

Maybe my smile wasn't nice enough, my nails not long enough, I was not successful enough, or my body not shapely enough. The list goes on and on. Again, it's amazing what peace will do. I'm so far beyond those doubts and negative thoughts. I am enough, always was.

I looked up to other people who were further along in life. In doing so, I felt more and more pressured, embarrassed, and depressed. It took me a while to realize that I was not only looking up to them but also comparing myself. I envied them. It wasn't that I wanted what they had but the happiness that they seemingly felt.

What I failed to realize and just could not see was their journey. I have no idea what all they had to go through to get to where they are. If they struggled as I did. I only saw the outcome and what was being portrayed for the public eye. I didn't know the real.

As I have been told many times before as well from others on the outside looking in. People often times see me and say that I am always smiling, bubbly, and helpful. That I am always motivating and guiding others. Again, It came naturally so I never really noticed it. It was simply who I was.

People were drawn to me, never realizing how much pain I was in. No one ever noticed the many times I would be fighting back tears while trying to make it through the day. No one saw me but I always saw and empathized with them. I was always there. I saw it as one of my flaws until I learned and enforced my boundaries.

Oh my, the growth. The peace. I no longer fight my feelings and tears. I embrace them and decide to push through. Slow down but never stop. I will walk in my light, in my truth, in my peace. That little, unnoticed girl that I thought that I once was, she'd be proud. She would now be able to pass on the knowledge and blessings that were given to her. She can now look into the mirror and see a woman, strong and true. I can live with that. I am most definitely at peace with it. I was so embarrassed when this came to my realization. Embarrassed that I hadn't learned it earlier on and also because I learned it from someone I barely knew. Then I smiled. I am so grateful for it all. I needed it and God delivered. None of this is a complaint, but a Testimony!

I have asked myself why I was so weak and repeatedly being taught these lessons. One of the first steps in gaining my peace was accepting that I am not a victim. I speak it daily. I AM NOT A VICTIM. I am a warrior! Though I'd walked through the darkness, was burned by the fire, and drowned in the waters, I AM NOT A VICTIM. I played a role in my lessons. No, of course not all of them but there were times where I allowed things that should not have been.

I was not careful nor mindful. I accepted the intolerable. I went along with what I should have ended, and often times never should have allowed to start. I accept responsibility in what has happened and I now know better. What did I lack? My knowledge of strength and control. I gave others control over my emotions, reactions, and situations where I held all of the cards. I just did not know how to play the game.

So, I felt repeatedly buried but I was wrong. I was simply a caterpillar being placed in my cocoon. The issue was that I never allowed myself to take on my new form. I was hearing but wasn't listening. I was seeing but not understanding, experiencing but not thriving. I hadn't learned what I needed to and therefore came back out a caterpillar. Now, finally, I am ready. This caterpillar has come out a butterfly, ready to spread her wings and soar.

You are here for a purpose. You have found peace, strength, and inspiration. Walk in your truth.

FADED VOICES

Self-Empowerment

I am strong, bold, and beautiful,

I can overcome anything with no problem,

No one can hurt me nor bring me down,

I deserve the best and shall receive it.

The enemy is no threat to me,

God is my all and will never let me fall,

God is my backbone, my cane, my right and, left hand man,

I am capable of all things and will not fail,

I cannot fail; if I fall, I will stand back on my feet

I am at peace, calm and warm,

No fears, no stress, and no worries.

I am loved and cared for,

I love myself first, as well as forgive myself.

I can and will make a difference,

I am somebody and am important,

I do matter and I have a purpose.

No one else is better than me; We are created equal.

I deserve the best and shall receive it.

No one can hurt me nor bring me down,

I can overcome any obstacle with no problem,

I am strong, bold, and beautiful.

Self-Empowerment

Uniquely Me

In life we struggle to find ourselves,

Who we are or who we want to be,

Someone once asked me what type of girl I am,

I answered, "I am simply me."

Back then, I didn't know who I was,

My confusion is now gone and now I know,

I am not her, she, them or we,

I am uniquely me!

I fall into no one's category,

I am no one's type of woman,

Refusing to be treated any kind of way,

Oh yeah, that's me,

I am not her, she, them or we,

I am uniquely me!

Playing games, lying, stealing, and hurting,

Honey, tricks are for kids,

Refusing to fall for it all,

Oh yeah, that's me,

So, the next time someone asks,

FADED VOICES

Wondering, curious about who I am,

I'll proudly stand up and say,

I am not her, she, them or we,

I am uniquely me!

Uniquely Me

Broken Chain

A broken house is not a home,

A broken group of relatives is not a family,

Fighting, arguing, lying and stealing,

No peace, no care, no respect, and no love,

A broken chain unable to be linked.

Corrupt minds and confused hearts,

Blind to the light; misguided and gone astray,

Erroneous ways stain a clear path,

Tear drops are left to soil the pain,

Waves of ambiguity and dread cloud the skies,

An abandoned hand forced to go without an embrace,

Open arms left to hold themselves; an empty space,

Strength and hope seem far from reach but much needed,

The innocent lives of others ruined in the crossfire,

A young child, defenseless against the world,

The family needed to help and support,
never shows.

Another lost soul enters in the world,

Unable to show or share what has not been
shown unto them,

This broken chain regrettably continues,
unable to be linked,

Cold blood passed down through the
generations,

Where does it end and how?

It's funny, a family can become a broken
chain.

Broken Chain

Lost Girl, Powerful Mission

A girl enters into the world,

Alone, no one there to guide her,

She is confused, lost, but on a mission,

Her thirst is her drive, her energy, her passion,

Left and right, far and near, lust follows her,

Men come to her, looking for riches,

Wanting to leave with them but not with her heart,

What does she do? Where does she go?

She just keeps walking, keeps moving, keeps pushing,

The games, lies, tricks, all thrown her way,

She never had a father to tell or show her real true love,

Her mother left her confused, to learn for herself,

To wander the streets of the world,

Filled with lust, heart break, fear, and pain,

He tries to touch her, to have her,

He says he loves her; this is how he proves it,

"Let me have you. I'll never hurt you."- he says.

"Everyone's doing it. Don't you want to feel good?" -he asks her.

He feels nothing for her, doesn't love her, doesn't care.

A girl enters the world,

All alone, no one there to guide her,

She's confused, lost, but on a mission,

Her thirst is her drive, her energy, her passion,

Left and right, far and near, lust follows her,

Mean come to her, looking for her riches,

Wanting to leave with them but not with her heart,

What does she do? Where does she go?

He lies there next to her, ready for her,

He kisses her here, there, her neck, her cheeks, her lips,

He touches her, her waist, her thighs, her stomach,

She begins to shiver, shaking
uncontrollably,

Her mind races, her heart pumps louder than
she can think,

Faster and faster her heart bleeds and races,

She's scared, he's still touching her, about to
take her,

She starts screaming and kicking, "No I
can't, I don't want this! Get off of me! Don't
touch me! What are you doing? Move! Get
away from me!"-she yells.

Her mind screams "Go" while her heart
screams the same.

She jumps up, puts back on her clothes, and
leaves.

Running scared, all alone in the streets of
the world,

He chases her but she gets away,

"Why me? Why is this happening? I'm so
confused, so lost."

Tears flow down her face, burning with
intensity and fear,

The pain follows and the tears continue,

A girl enters into the world,

FADED VOICES

Alone, no one there to guide her,

She's confused, lost but on a mission,

Her thirst is her drive, her energy, her passion,

Left and right, far and near, lust follows her,

Men come to her, looking for her riches,

Wanting to leave with them but not with her heart,

What does she do? Where does she go?

Time passes, she still holds her riches, her gold,

Another comes, he tries her, only to be denied,

He tries to rape her, but this time she is ready; prepared.

He loses, she takes her riches and keeps moving,

Feeling stronger but still lost, still on a mission,

She's in college now, one day to be questioned,

Her professor asks her, "What are you looking for?"

"I don't know but I have to find it"- she says.

She leaves, time passes. She decides to join a church.

One day after service, the pastor stops her.

"You've found God and I'm proud of you."

She says, "You're right. I have found God and I thank you. I am trying to find myself now."

The pastor hugs her and says "you've overcome every obstacle in your life. You've become a very successful young woman as well."

The girl stops to think. "You know what, I've been looking for myself this entire time not realizing I'd found me. I am strong and I am still here. I do know who I am, I'm a child of God."

A girl entered into the world,

All alone, no one there to guide her,

She was confused, lost, but completed her mission,

Her thirst was her drive, her energy, her passion,

Left and right, far and near lust followed
her,

Men came to her, looking for her riches,

Wanting to leave with them but not with her
heart,

What was she to do? Where was she to go?

She finds herself, loves herself, and she goes
to God.

She now knows what it feels like to have
real, true and unconditional love.

A girl entered the world, found herself, and
created an angel.

Lost Girl, Powerful Mission

Acknowledgements

First and foremost, I want to thank God. I could not have made it this far on my journey without Him and the strength and patience He has placed within me. I'm truly grateful for the experiences I've both endured and witnessed. They've taught me and mean more than I could ever fully know. There were times when I felt like giving up and I no longer wanted to be here. I felt worthless, unnoticed, and as if I was always struggling. When I was going through, I never thought I'd make it through but here I stand.

To my Pumpkins, you have saved my life in more ways than I could ever explain to you. Having you has helped me to heal my inner child and truly learn forgiveness and patience. I am incredibly grateful for you. Yes, you came through and shook things up a bit but you also helped me grow and see clearly. God truly knew what He was doing when

He sent me you. I love you so much.

I would also like to thank my brothers, for being my rock and giving me advice (even when it was not what I wanted to hear). We speak very often, they listen (sometimes lol), tell me like it is, and they really keep me going. We have gone through quite a bit, both together and separately. We will always be there for one another. We all have been through the ringer and I am so blessed to have you all as brothers. We have taught each other so much in many ways. We fuss and fight, as siblings do, but I wouldn't have it any other way. I love you guys.

Also, my best friends DeAnna and Kelvin. I want to thank DeAnna (who is more of a sister) for being there for me through my darkest times even while going through her own. DeAnna you are such a fighter. We may not speak everyday but we have always been there for each other. You are beautiful through and through. I will always be there for you.

Kelvin thank you for always having my back and being there during my tough times. You also went through your own rough patches but you never turn away someone in need. You are always there for everyone. A true friend. A great man. You stepped up for me when my dad passed away and it means more to me than you know. DeAnna and Kelvin, I greatly appreciate you both and wish you well.

Also, I have to thank my dad. He had become my human diary and the one person that I knew would not pass judgement. I was able to come to him and we could openly speak about anything. He really helped and guided me when I needed it most. Even though, at the time, I wasn't aware of it. I love you Dad and may you continue to rest in peace.

Thank you all! I love you and God bless.

About the Author

Serenity Aymala is a new author with her first book *Faded Voices.* Serenity has been writing both short stories and poetry since childhood. Both writing and fitness have been her lifelong forms of therapy. At a young age she came to realize that putting her experiences and emotions onto paper made her journey easier to embark on. She had gone through quite a bit in her life yet was always the person being there for others. Serenity was the "counselor" amongst friends and family. She went on to study Psychology/Marriage and Family Therapy in college. Ms. Aymala encourages others to write and remember that what cannot be said, can always be written.

Made in the USA
Columbia, SC
11 July 2022

63323904R00070